AMAZING AMERICANS
COUNTRY MUSIC STARS

# MIRANDA LAMBERT

**by Jim Gigliotti**

Consultant: Starshine Roshell
Music and Entertainment Journalist
Santa Barbara, California

BEARPORT
PUBLISHING

New York, New York

## Credits

Cover, © John Salangsang/Invision/AP Photo; 4, © AdMedia Inc./Sipa USA/Newscom; 5, © Nicolas Khayat/ ABACAUSA/Newscom; 6, Courtesy Seth Poppel Yearbook Library; 7, © Jason Moore/Zuma Press/Newscom; 8, Courtesy Seth Poppel Yearbook Library; 9, © Andre Jenny Stockconnection Worldwide/Newscom; 10, Courtesy Ken Carter; 11, © Tdovelaux816/Dreamstime; 12, © Jason Moore/Zuma Press/Newscom; 13, © Courtesy Nashville Star Press; 14, © Harrison McClary/Reuters/Newscom; 15, © Jason Moore/Zuma Press/Newscom; 16, © Featureflash/Dreamstime; 17, © Chris Pizzello/AP Photo; 18, © Michael Turner/Dreamstime; 19, © Krista Kennell/ABACA USA/Newscom; 20, Courtesy MadeFirst; 21, © MJT/AdMedia/Newscom; 22, © Jason Moore/ Zuma Press/Newscom; 23, © Andrey Kuzmin/Dreamstime.

Publisher: Kenn Goin
Creative Director: Spencer Brinker
Production and Photo Research: Shoreline Publishing Group LLC

*Library of Congress Cataloging-in-Publication Data*

Names: Gigliotti, Jim, author. | Roshell, Starshine.
Title: Miranda Lambert / by Jim Gigliotti ; consultant: Starshine Roshell.
Description: New York, New York : Bearport Publishing, [2019] | Series:
   Amazing Americans: Country music stars | Includes bibliographical
   references and index.
Identifiers: LCCN 2018014541 (print) | LCCN 2018016770 (ebook) |
   ISBN 9781684027309 (ebook) | ISBN 9781684026845 (library)
Subjects: LCSH: Lambert, Miranda, 1983–Juvenile literature. | Country
   musicians—United States—Biography—Juvenile literature.
Classification: LCC ML3930.L145 (ebook) | LCC ML3930.L145 G55 2019 (print) |
   DDC 782.421642092 [B] —dc23
LC record available at https://lccn.loc.gov/2018014541

For more information, write to Bearport Publishing Company, Inc., 45 West 21st Street, Suite 3B, New York, New York 10010. Printed in the United States of America.

10 9 8 7 6 5 4 3 2 1

# CONTENTS

# On Fire!

In 2005, Miranda Lambert sang her hit song "Kerosene" at a big awards show. As she performed, a wall of flames shot up behind her. The crowd went wild. If country fans hadn't known Miranda before, they knew her now!

Miranda also sang with country star Blake Shelton at the 2005 show.

4

The 2005 show was the *Country Music Association (CMA) Awards*. The show is held each year to honor country music stars.

# Texas Girl

Miranda Leigh Lambert was born in Longview, Texas, on November 10, 1983. Miranda, her parents, and her brother, Luke, loved music. The family often went to country music shows in Nashville, Tennessee. At home, they liked to sit on the porch as Miranda's father played the guitar.

**Miranda in sixth grade**

In 2017, Miranda sang at the same country show she had gone to as a kid.

Miranda's dad bought her a guitar when she was ten years old.

7

# Out of Her Shell

In grade school, Miranda was very shy. She hardly ever talked. In high school, she took a **debate** class. It really helped her with public speaking. Miranda's teacher also encouraged her to speak her mind. That gave Miranda a huge confidence boost and also helped with her singing!

Miranda singing and playing guitar as a high school senior

8

As a child, Miranda played shortstop on her town's Little League softball team.

# True to Herself

After high school, Miranda started singing at a club in her hometown. Later that year, she moved to Nashville. However, she didn't like the songs that people in the music business wanted her to sing. "I can't sell something that I don't believe," she said. Miranda moved back to Texas and decided to write her own music.

Miranda sang at this Longview, Texas, club.

Miranda recorded her first album, *Miranda Lambert*, in 2001. It was made before she ever **signed** with a record company.

# First Contract

In 2003, Miranda competed on *Nashville Star*, a TV talent show. Miranda finished third. However, one of the judges was an **executive** for Sony Music. She loved Miranda's singing and style. Before long, Miranda signed a record deal. She was thrilled!

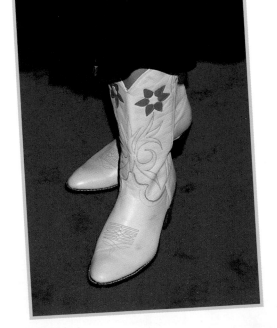

**Miranda wearing a favorite pair of cowboy boots**

Miranda singing on *Nashville Star* in 2003

*Nashville Star* was on TV from 2003 to 2008. It launched the careers of many country music stars.

# Top of the Charts

In 2005, Miranda released her first album, *Kerosene.* The album reached number one on *Billboard* magazine's country music chart. Soon, Miranda began touring with some of country music's biggest stars! She opened shows for Dierks Bentley, George Strait, and Keith Urban.

Miranda mostly performs **solo**. However, she also sings with the popular **trio** Pistol Annies.

Miranda almost always plays a pink guitar. Here she sings at a Nashville show in 2012.

# Songwriter

Miranda's next album, *Crazy Ex-Girlfriend*, came out in 2007. It was such a success that Miranda was soon **headlining** her own tours. She was also writing most of her songs. One special song was "Over You." She wrote it with Blake Shelton, who was her husband from 2011 to 2015. They wrote the song to honor Blake's brother, Chris, who had died.

**Miranda and Blake Shelton**

After 2017, Miranda released several best-selling albums. These included *Revolution*, *Four the Record*, and *Platinum*.

*Platinum* won Miranda a 2015 Grammy Award for best country album.

# Animal Lover

Along with writing music, Miranda loves helping animals. She has seven rescue dogs at home! In 2009, she started MuttNation to help homeless animals. In 2017, Hurricane Harvey hit Texas. MuttNation rushed in to help rescue pets.

Miranda enjoys riding horses, too. She races them around barrels on a twisty course.

Miranda snuggles
with a pup in 2013.

# Country Superstar!

Miranda is best known for pouring her feelings into her songs. "I figure, if I'm feeling something, other people are, too," she says. In 2018, she was the Academy of Country Music's (ACM) Female Vocalist of the Year—for the ninth year in a row! This shy girl has become a superstar!

Miranda's trailer

Miranda brings her own trailer wherever she goes. It has a giant tiara on top!

Miranda with her ACM awards in 2018

# Timeline

**Here are some key dates in Miranda Lambert's life.**

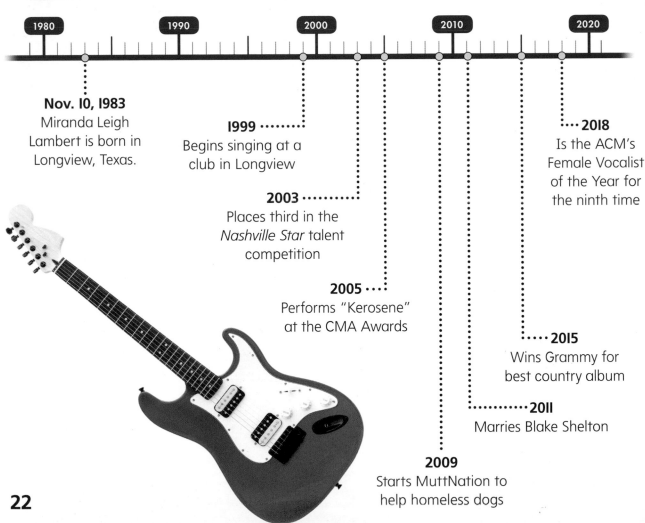

1980 — 1990 — 2000 — 2010 — 2020

**Nov. 10, 1983**
Miranda Leigh Lambert is born in Longview, Texas.

**1999**
Begins singing at a club in Longview

**2003**
Places third in the *Nashville Star* talent competition

**2005**
Performs "Kerosene" at the CMA Awards

**2009**
Starts MuttNation to help homeless dogs

**2011**
Marries Blake Shelton

**2015**
Wins Grammy for best country album

**2018**
Is the ACM's Female Vocalist of the Year for the ninth time

# Glossary

**debate** (di-BATE) a discussion between two sides that have opposite views about an issue

**executive** (eg-ZEK-yuh-tiv) a person who helps run a company

**headlining** (HED-line-ing) appearing as the main performer in a show

**signed** (SINED) agreed to produce music for a company in exchange for money

**solo** (SOH-loh) alone

**tiara** (tee-AH-ruh) a jeweled crown

**trio** (TREE-oh) a group of three

# Index

# Read More

**Franke, Aife.** *Miranda Lambert (Country Music Stars).* New York: Gareth Stevens (2011).

**Tieck, Sarah.** *Miranda Lambert: Country Music Star (Big Buddy Biographies).* Edina, MN: ABDO (2012).

# Learn More Online

To learn more about Miranda Lambert, visit
**www.bearportpublishing.com/AmazingAmericans**

# About the Author

Jim Gigliotti is a former editor at the National Football League. He now writes books on a variety of topics for young readers.